EIGHTY-NINTH EDITION

Manual of The Mother Church
The First Church of Christ
Scientist
in Boston, Massachusetts

by

MARY BAKER EDDY

*Discoverer and Founder of Christian Science
and Author of
Science and Health with Key to the Scriptures*

Marcas Registradas

Published by

THE FIRST CHURCH OF CHRIST, SCIENTIST

in Boston, Massachusetts, U.S.A.

EXTRACT FROM A LETTER IN "MISCELLANEOUS WRITINGS"   *By Mary Baker Eddy*

THE Rules and By-Laws in the Manual of The First Church of Christ, Scientist, Boston, originated not in solemn conclave as in ancient Sanhedrim. They were not arbitrary opinions nor dictatorial demands, such as one person might impose on another. They were impelled by a power not one's own, were written at different dates, and as the occasion required. They sprang from necessity, the logic of events,—from the immediate demand for them as a help that must be supplied to maintain the dignity and defense of our Cause; hence their simple, scientific basis, and detail so requisite to demonstrate genuine Christian Science, and which will do for the race what absolute doctrines destined for future generations might not accomplish.

Table of Contents

Church By-Laws

CHURCH OFFICERS

CHURCH MEMBERSHIP

DISCIPLINE

MEETINGS

CHURCH SERVICES

READING ROOMS   ART. XXI

RELATION AND DUTIES OF
MEMBERS TO PASTOR EMERITUS   ART. XXII

THE MOTHER CHURCH
AND BRANCH CHURCHES   ART. XXIII

GUARDIANSHIP OF
CHURCH FUNDS ART. XXIV

THE CHRISTIAN SCIENCE
PUBLISHING SOCIETY ART. XXV

TEACHING CHRISTIAN SCIENCE

TEACHERS. ART. XXVI

BOARD OF EDUCATION

BOARD OF LECTURESHIP

Appendix

Tenets

of The Mother Church
The First Church of Christ, Scientist

To be signed by those uniting with The First 1
Church of Christ, Scientist, in Boston, Mass.

1. As adherents of Truth, we take the inspired 3
Word of the Bible as our sufficient guide to eternal
Life.

2. We acknowledge and adore one supreme and 6
infinite God. We acknowledge His Son, one Christ;
the Holy Ghost or divine Comforter; and man in
God's image and likeness. 9

3. We acknowledge God's forgiveness of sin in
the destruction of sin and the spiritual understanding
that casts out evil as unreal. But the belief in sin is 12
punished so long as the belief lasts.

4. We acknowledge Jesus' atonement as the evidence of divine, efficacious Love, unfolding man's 15
unity with God through Christ Jesus the Way-shower;

1 and we acknowledge that man is saved through Christ,
through Truth, Life, and Love as demonstrated by the
3 Galilean Prophet in healing the sick and overcoming
sin and death.

5. We acknowledge that the crucifixion of Jesus
6 and his resurrection served to uplift faith to understand eternal Life, even the allness of Soul, Spirit, and
the nothingness of matter.

9   6. And we solemnly promise to watch, and pray
for that Mind to be in us which was also in Christ
Jesus; to do unto others as we would have them do
12 unto us; and to be merciful, just, and pure.

MARY BAKER EDDY

Historical Sketch

IN THE spring of 1879, a little band of earnest
seekers after Truth went into deliberations over
forming a church without creeds, to be called the
"CHURCH OF CHRIST, SCIENTIST." They were members of evangelical churches, and students of Mrs.
Mary Baker Eddy in Christian Science, and were
known as "Christian Scientists."

At a meeting of the Christian Scientist Association,
April 12, 1879, on motion of Mrs. Eddy, it was
voted, — To organize a church designed to com-
memorate the word and works of our Master, which
should reinstate primitive Christianity and its lost
element of healing.

Mrs. Eddy was appointed on the committee to
draft the Tenets of The Mother Church — the chief
corner stone whereof is, that Christian Science, as
taught and demonstrated by our Master, casts out
error, heals the sick, and restores the lost Israel:

1 for "the stone which the builders rejected, the same is become the head of the corner."

3   The charter for the Church was obtained June, 1879,* and the same month the members, twenty-six in number, extended a call to Mary Baker Eddy
6 to become their pastor. She accepted the call, and was ordained A. D. 1881. Although walking through deep waters, the little Church went steadily
9 on, increasing in numbers, and at every epoch saying,

   "Hitherto hath the Lord helped us."

12   On the twenty-third day of September, 1892, at the request of Rev. Mary Baker Eddy, twelve of her students and Church members met and re-
15 organized, under her jurisdiction, the Christian Science Church and named it, THE FIRST CHURCH OF CHRIST, SCIENTIST.

18   At this meeting twenty others of Mrs. Eddy's students and members of her former Church were elected members of this Church, — those with others
21 that have since been elected were known as "First Members." The Church Tenets, Rules, and By-Laws, as prepared by Mrs. Eddy, were adopted. A
24 By-Law adopted March 17, 1903, changed the title of "First Members" to "Executive Members." (On July 8, 1908, the By-Laws pertaining to "Ex-
27 ecutive Members" were repealed.)

THE FIRST CHURCH OF CHRIST, SCIENTIST, IN BOS- 1
TON, MASS., is designed to be built on the Rock,
Christ; even the understanding and demonstration 3
of divine Truth, Life, and Love, healing and saving
the world from sin and death; thus to reflect in some
degree the Church Universal and Triumphant.   6

* Steps were taken to promote the Church of Christ, Scientist, in April,
May and June; formal organization was accomplished and the charter
obtained in August, 1879.

CHURCH OFFICERS

Rev. MARY BAKER EDDY
Pastor Emeritus

ↄↄ

Christian Science Board of Directors
DeWITT JOHN
CHARLES LOUIS REILLY
HARVEY W. WOOD
Mrs. JEAN STARK HEBENSTREIT
HAL M. FRIESEN

ↄↄ

JOHN R. PETERSON
President

BRYAN G. POPE
First Reader
Conducts services and reads from the Christian Science textbook,
"SCIENCE AND HEALTH WITH KEY TO THE
SCRIPTURES"
By Mary Baker Eddy

Mrs. VIRGINIA NICHOLS CHANCEY
Second Reader
Reads from the SCRIPTURES

ROBERT H. MITCHELL
Clerk
Christian Science Center, Boston, Mass.

MARC ENGELER
Treasurer
Christian Science Center, Boston, Mass.

June, 1978—June, 1979

Church By-Laws

Church By-Laws

Article I
NAMES, ELECTION, AND DUTIES

Names. SECTION 1. The Church officers shall consist of the Pastor Emeritus, a Board of Directors, a President, a Clerk, a Treasurer, and two Readers.

President. SECT. 2. The President shall be elected, subject to the approval of the Pastor Emeritus, by the Board of Directors[1] on Monday preceding the annual meeting of the Church. The President shall hold office for one year, and the same person is eligible for election but once in three years.

Clerk and Treasurer. SECT. 3. The term of office for the Clerk and the Treasurer of this

[1] See under "Deed of Trust" for incorporation of the "Christian Science Board of Directors."

25

Church (also for the editors and the manager
of The Christian Science Publishing Society,
and the manager of the general Committee on
Publication in Boston) is one year each, dating
from the time of election to office. Incumbents
who have served one year or more, may be re-
elected, or new officers elected, at the annual
meeting held for this purpose, by a unanimous
vote of the Christian Science Board of Directors and the consent of the Pastor Emeritus
given in her own handwriting.

Readers.   SECT. 4.   Every third year Readers shall be elected in The Mother Church by
the Board of Directors, which shall inform the
Pastor Emeritus of the names of its candidates
before they are elected; and if she objects, said
candidates shall not be chosen. The Directors
shall fix the salaries of the Readers.

Directors.   SECT. 5.   The Christian Science
Board of Directors shall consist of five members.
They shall fill a vacancy occurring on that Board
after the candidate is approved by the Pastor
Emeritus.   A majority vote or the request of
Mrs. Eddy shall dismiss a member.   Members
shall neither report the discussions of this Board,
nor those with Mrs. Eddy.

Church Business. SECT. 6. The business of The Mother Church shall be transacted by its Christian Science Board of Directors. The manager of the general Committee on Publication in the United States shall order no special action to be taken by said Committee that is not named in the Manual of this Church without consulting with the full Board of Directors of The Mother Church and receiving the written consent of said Board.

Publishing Buildings. SECT. 7. It shall be the duty of the Christian Science Board of Directors to provide a suitable building for the publication of *The Christian Science Journal, Christian Science Sentinel, Der Herold der Christian Science,* and all other Christian Science literature published by The Christian Science Publishing Society. It shall also be the duty of the Christian Science Board of Directors to provide suitable rooms, conveniently and pleasantly located in the same building, for the publication and sale of the books of which Mary Baker Eddy is, or may be, the author, and of other literature connected therewith.

Trusteeships and Syndicates. SECT. 8. Boards of Trustees and Syndicates may be

1 formed by The Mother Church, subject to the
approval of the Pastor Emeritus.

3 **Duties of Church Officers.** SECT. 9. Law
constitutes government, and disobedience to the
laws of The Mother Church must ultimate in
6 annulling its Tenets and By-Laws. Without a
proper system of government and form of action, nations, individuals, and religion are un-
9 protected; hence the necessity of this By-Law
and the warning of Holy Writ: "That servant,
which knew his lord's will, and prepared not
12 himself, neither did according to his will, shall
be beaten with many stripes."

It is the duty of the Christian Science Board of
15 Directors to watch and make sure that the officers of this Church perform the functions of
their several offices promptly and well. If an
18 officer fails to fulfil all the obligations of his
office, the Board of Directors shall immediately
call a meeting and notify this officer either to
21 resign his place or to perform his office faithfully; then failing to do either, said officer shall
be dismissed from this Church, and his dismis-
24 sal shall be written on the Church records.

It is the duty of any member of this Church,
and especially of one who has been or who is

the First Reader of a church, to inform the
Board of Directors of the failure of the Committee on Publication or of any other officer in
this Church to perform his official duties.   A
Director shall not make known the name of the
complainant.

If the Christian Science Board of Directors fails
to fulfil the requirements of this By-Law, and a
member of this Church or the Pastor Emeritus
shall complain thereof to the Clerk and the complaint be found valid, the Directors shall resign
their office or perform their functions faithfully.
Failing to do thus, the Pastor Emeritus shall appoint five suitable members of this Church to fill
the vacancy.   The salary of the members of the
Board of Directors shall be at present two thousand five hundred dollars each annually.

Article II

READERS OF THE MOTHER CHURCH

Election.   SECTION 1.   The Readers for The
Mother Church shall be a man and a woman,
one to read the BIBLE, and one to read SCIENCE
AND HEALTH WITH KEY TO THE SCRIPTURES.

1   **Eligibility.**   SECT. 2.   The Directors shall
select intelligible Readers who are exemplary
3 Christians and good English scholars.   They
must be members of The Mother Church.

Removal.   SECT. 3.   If a Reader in The
6 Mother Church be found at any time inadequate
or unworthy, he or she shall be removed from
office by a majority vote of the Board of Di-
9 rectors and the consent of the Pastor Emeritus,
and the vacancy supplied.

First Reader's Residence.   SECT. 4.   Unless
12 Mrs. Eddy requests otherwise, the First Reader
of The Mother Church shall occupy, during his
term of Readership, the house of the Pastor
15 Emeritus, No. 385 Commonwealth Avenue, Boston.   The Board of Directors shall pay from
the Church funds the taxes and rent on this
18 property;   the Board shall attend to the insur-
ance before it expires, suitably furnish the
house, and keep the property in good repair, so
21 long as Mrs. Eddy does not occupy the house
herself and the occupants are satisfactory to
her.

Article III   1

DUTIES OF READERS OF THE MOTHER CHURCH AND OF ITS BRANCH CHURCHES   3

Moral Obligations. SECTION 1. The Readers of The Mother Church and of all its branch churches must devote a suitable portion of their 6 time to preparation for the reading of the Sunday lesson, — a lesson on which the prosperity of Christian Science largely depends. They must 9 keep themselves unspotted from the world, — uncontaminated with evil, — that the mental atmosphere they exhale shall promote health and 12 holiness, even that spiritual *animus* so universally needed.

First Readers' Duties. SECT. 2. It shall be 15 the duty of the First Readers to conduct the principal part of the Sunday services, and the Wednesday evening meetings.   18

Suitable Selections. SECT. 3. The First Readers shall read, as a part of the Wednesday evening services, selections from the SCRIPTURES, 21 and from SCIENCE AND HEALTH WITH KEY TO THE SCRIPTURES.

1   **Order of Reading.** SECT. 4. The First Readers in the Christian Science churches shall read
3 the correlative texts in SCIENCE AND HEALTH WITH KEY TO THE SCRIPTURES; and the Second Readers shall read the BIBLE texts. The readings
6 from the SCRIPTURES shall precede the readings from SCIENCE AND HEALTH. The Readers shall not read from copies or manuscripts, but from
9 the books.

Naming Book and Author. SECT. 5. The Readers of SCIENCE AND HEALTH WITH KEY TO
12 THE SCRIPTURES, before commencing to read from this book, shall distinctly announce the full title of the book and give the author's name.
15 Such announcement shall be made but once during the lesson.

Readers in Branch Churches. SECT. 6.
18 These Readers shall be members of The Mother Church. They shall read understandingly and be well educated. They shall make no remarks
21 explanatory of the LESSON-SERMON at any time, but they shall read all notices and remarks that may be printed in the CHRISTIAN SCIENCE QUAR-
24 TERLY. This By-Law applies to Readers in all the branch churches.

Enforcement of By-Laws. SECT. 7. It shall

be the duty of every member of The Mother 1
Church, who is a First Reader in a Church of
Christ, Scientist, to enforce the discipline and 3
by-laws of the church in which he is Reader.

A Reader not a Leader. SECT. 8. The Church
Reader shall not be a Leader, but he shall main- 6
tain the Tenets, Rules, and discipline of the
Church. A Reader shall not be a President of
a church.   9

CHURCH MEMBERSHIP

Article IV

QUALIFICATIONS FOR MEMBERSHIP

Believe in Christian Science. SECTION 1. To become a member of The Mother Church, The First Church of Christ, Scientist, in Boston, Mass., the applicant must be a believer in the doctrines of Christian Science, according to the platform and teaching contained in the Christian Science textbook, SCIENCE AND HEALTH WITH KEY TO THE SCRIPTURES, by Rev. Mary Baker Eddy. The BIBLE, together with SCIENCE AND HEALTH and other works by Mrs. Eddy, shall be his only textbooks for self-instruction in Christian Science, and for teaching and practising metaphysical healing.

Free from Other Denominations. SECT. 2. This Church will receive a member of another Church of Christ, Scientist, but not a church member from a different denomination until that membership is dissolved.

Children when Twelve Years Old. SECT. 3. 1
Children who have arrived at the age of twelve
years, who are approved, and whose applications 3
are countersigned by one of Mrs. Eddy's loyal students, by a Director, or by a student of the Board
of Education, may be admitted to membership 6
with The Mother Church.

Article V

APPLICATIONS FOR MEMBERSHIP   9

Students of the College. SECTION 1. Applications for membership with The Mother Church
from students of the Massachusetts Metaphysical 12
College who studied with Rev. Mary Baker Eddy,
shall be signed by the Christian Science Board
of Directors as evidence of the loyalty of the 15
applicants.

Other Students. SECT. 2. Applicants for
membership who have not studied Christian Sci- 18
ence with Rev. Mary Baker Eddy, can unite
with this Church only by approval from students
of Mrs. Eddy, loyal to the teachings of the text- 21
book, SCIENCE AND HEALTH WITH KEY TO THE

1 SCRIPTURES, or from members of The Mother
Church, as provided in Article VI, Sect. 2, of
3 these By-Laws.

Students' Pupils. SECT. 3. Applications for
membership with The Mother Church, coming
6 from pupils of loyal students who have taken
the Primary or Normal Course at the Massachusetts Metaphysical College or in the Board
9 of Education, or from pupils of those who have
passed an examination by the Board of Education, shall have the approval and signature of
12 their teachers, except in such cases as are provided for in Sect. 4 of this Article.

Exceptional Cases. SECT. 4. Loyal Chris-
15 tian Scientists whose teachers are deceased, absent, or disloyal, — or those whose teachers, for
insufficient cause, refuse to endorse their appli-
18 cations for membership with The Mother Church,
— can apply to the Clerk of this Church, and
present to him a recommendation signed by three
21 members thereof in good standing, after which,
the unanimous vote of the Board of Directors
may admit said applicant to membership.

24 **Addressed to Clerk.** SECT. 5. All applications for membership must be addressed to the
Clerk of the Church.

Endorsing Applications. SECT. 6. A member of The Mother Church shall not endorse nor countersign an application for membership therewith until after the blank has been properly filled out by an applicant. A member who violates this By-Law shall be disciplined.

Notice of Rejection. SECT. 7. If an application for membership with The First Church of Christ, Scientist, in Boston, Mass., is rejected, the Clerk of the Church shall send to the applicant a notice of such rejection; but neither the Clerk nor the Church shall be obliged to report the cause for rejection.

Article VI
RECOMMENDATION AND ELECTION

Pupils of Normal Students. SECTION 1. One Normal student cannot recommend the pupil of another Normal student, so long as both are loyal to their Leader and to the Christian Science textbook, except as provided for in Article V, Sect. 4.

Members of The Mother Church. SECT. 2. Only members of The Mother Church are quali-

1 fied to approve for membership individuals who
are known to them to be Christians, and faith-
3 ful, loyal students of the textbook, SCIENCE AND
HEALTH WITH KEY TO THE SCRIPTURES. If the
approver is not a loyal student of Mrs. Eddy, a
6 Director of this Church, or a student of the Board
of Education who holds a degree, the application
must be countersigned by one of these.

9   **Election.** SECT. 3. Applicants for membership in this Church, whose applications are
correctly prepared, may be elected by majority
12 vote of the Christian Science Board of Directors at the semi-annual meetings held for this
purpose.

15   Article VII
                PROBATIONARY MEMBERSHIP

Members who once Withdrew. SECTION 1.
18 Individuals who have heretofore been members
of this Church, or were members of the Church
of Christ, Scientist, organized in 1879 by Mary
21 Baker Eddy, but who have voluntarily with-
drawn, may be received into this Church on one
year's probation, provided they are willing and

anxious to live according to its requirements and make application for membership according to its By-Laws.   If, at the expiration of said one year, they are found worthy, they shall be received into full membership, but if not found worthy their applications shall be void.

Members once Dismissed.   SECT. 2.   A full member or a probationary member, who has been excommunicated once, and who afterward, when sufficient time has elapsed thoroughly to test his sincerity, gives due evidence of having genuinely repented and of being radically reformed, shall be eligible to probationary membership upon a unanimous vote of the Christian Science Board of Directors.

Ineligible for Probation.   SECT. 3.   If a member has been twice notified of his excommunication, he shall not again be received into this Church.

1   **DISCIPLINE**

Article VIII

3   GUIDANCE OF MEMBERS

A Rule for Motives and Acts.   SECTION 1.
Neither animosity nor mere personal attachment
6 should impel the motives or acts of the members
of The Mother Church. In Science, divine Love
alone governs man; and a Christian Scientist
9 reflects the sweet amenities of Love, in rebuk-
ing sin, in true brotherliness, charitableness, and
forgiveness. The members of this Church should
12 daily watch and pray to be delivered from
all evil, from prophesying, judging, condemning, counseling, influencing or being influenced
15 erroneously.

To be Read in Church.   SECT. 2.   The
above Church Rule shall be read in The Mother
18 Church and in the branch churches by the First
Reader on the first Sunday of each month.
On Communion day the Church Tenets are to
21 be read.

Christ Jesus the Ensample.   SECT. 3.   He
who dated the Christian era is the Ensample in
Christian Science.   Careless comparison or irrev-
erent reference to Christ Jesus is abnormal in a
Christian Scientist, and is prohibited.   When it is
necessary to show the great gulf between Christian Science and theosophy, hypnotism, or spiritualism, do it, but without hard words.   The wise
man saith, "A soft answer turneth away wrath."
However despitefully used and misrepresented
by the churches or the press, in return employ
no violent invective, and do good unto your
enemies when the opportunity occurs.   A departure from this rule disqualifies a member for
office in the Church or on the Board of Lectureship, and renders this member liable to discipline and, possibly, dismissal from The Mother
Church.

Daily Prayer.   SECT. 4.   It shall be the duty
of every member of this Church to pray each
day: "Thy kingdom come;"   let the reign of
divine Truth, Life, and Love be established in
me, and rule out of me all sin;   and may Thy
Word enrich the affections of all mankind, and
govern them!

1 **Prayer in Church.** SECT. 5. The prayers in Christian Science churches shall be offered for
3 the congregations collectively and exclusively.

Alertness to Duty. SECT. 6. It shall be the duty of every member of this Church to defend
6 himself daily against aggressive mental sugges- tion, and not be made to forget nor to neglect his duty to God, to his Leader, and to mankind.
9 By his works he shall be judged, — and justified or condemned.

One Christ. SECT. 7. In accordance with
12 the Christian Science textbooks, — the BIBLE, and SCIENCE AND HEALTH WITH KEY TO THE SCRIPTURES, — and in accord with all of Mrs.
15 Eddy's teachings, members of this Church shall neither entertain a belief nor signify a belief in more than one Christ, even that Christ whereof
18 the Scripture beareth testimony.

No Malpractice. SECT. 8. Members will not intentionally or knowingly mentally malpractise,
21 inasmuch as Christian Science can only be prac- tised according to the Golden Rule: "All things whatsoever ye would that men should do to you,
24 do ye even so to them." (Matt. 7:12.)

A member of The Mother Church who men- tally malpractises upon or treats our Leader or

her staff without her or their consent shall be dis- 1
ciplined, and a second offense as aforesaid shall
cause the name of said member to be dropped 3
forever from The Mother Church.

Formulas Forbidden. SECT. 9. No member
shall use written formulas, nor permit his patients 6
or pupils to use them, as auxiliaries to teaching Christian Science or for healing the sick.
Whatever is requisite for either is contained in 9
the books of the Discoverer and Founder of
Christian Science. Sometimes she may strengthen
the faith by a written text as no one else can. 12

No Adulterating Christian Science. SECT. 10.
A member of this Church shall not publish
profuse quotations from Mary Baker Eddy's 15
copyrighted works without her permission, and
shall not plagiarize her writings. This By-Law
not only calls more serious attention to the com- 18
mandment of the Decalogue, but tends to prevent Christian Science from being *adulterated.*

No Incorrect Literature. SECT. 11. A mem- 21
ber of this Church shall neither buy, sell, nor circulate Christian Science literature which is not
correct in its statement of the divine Principle 24
and rules and the demonstration of Christian
Science. Also the spirit in which the writer

1 has written his literature shall be definitely considered.   His writings must show strict adher-
3 ence to the Golden Rule, or his literature shall
not be adjudged Christian Science. A departure
from the spirit or letter of this By-Law involves
6 schisms in our Church and the possible loss, for
a time, of Christian Science.

Obnoxious Books.   SECT. 12.   A member of
9 this Church shall not patronize a publishing
house or bookstore that has for sale obnoxious
books.

12 **Per Capita Tax.**   SECT. 13.   Every member
of The Mother Church shall pay annually a per
capita tax of not less than one dollar, which shall
15 be forwarded each year to the Church Treasurer.

Church Periodicals.   SECT. 14.   It shall be the
privilege and duty of every member, who can
18 afford it, to subscribe for the periodicals which
are the organs of this Church; and it shall be
the duty of the Directors to see that these period-
21 icals are ably edited and kept abreast of the
times.

Church Organizations Ample.   SECT. 15.
24 Members of this Church shall not unite with
organizations which impede their progress in
Christian Science. God requires our whole heart,

and He supplies within the wide channels of The
Mother Church dutiful and sufficient occupation
for all its members.

Joining Another Society.   SECT. 16.   It shall
be the duty of the members of The Mother
Church and of its branches to promote peace on
earth and good will toward men; but members
of The Mother Church shall not hereafter become members of other societies except those
specified in The Mother Church Manual, and
they shall strive to promote the welfare of all
mankind by demonstrating the rules of divine
Love.

Forbidden Membership.   SECT. 17.   A member of The First Church of Christ, Scientist, in
Boston, Mass., shall not be a member of any
church whose Readers are not Christian Scientists
and members of The Mother Church.

Officious Members.   SECT. 18.   A member of
The Mother Church is not entitled to hold office
or read in branch churches of this denomination
except by invitation.

Legal Titles.   SECT. 19.   Students of Christian Science must drop the titles of Reverend and
Doctor, except those who have received these
titles under the *laws* of the *State.*

Illegal Adoption. SECT. 20. No person shall be a member of this Church who claims a spiritually adopted child or a spiritually adopted husband or wife. There must be legal adoption and legal marriage, which can be verified according to the laws of our land.

Use of Initials "C. S." SECT. 21. A member of The Mother Church shall not place the initials "C. S." after his name on circulars, cards, or leaflets, which advertise his business or profession, except as a Christian Science practitioner.

Practitioners and Patients. SECT. 22. Members of this Church shall hold in sacred confidence all private communications made to them by their patients; also such information as may come to them by reason of their relation of practitioner to patient. A failure to do this shall subject the offender to Church discipline.

A member of The Mother Church shall not, under pardonable circumstances, sue his patient for recovery of payment for said member's practice, on penalty of discipline and liability to have his name removed from membership. Also he shall reasonably reduce his price in chronic cases of recovery, and in cases where he has not effected a cure. A Christian Scientist is a humanitarian; he is benevolent, forgiving, long-suffering, and seeks to overcome evil with good.

Duty to Patients. SECT. 23. If a member of this Church has a patient whom he does not heal, and whose case he cannot fully diagnose, he may consult with an M. D. on the anatomy involved. And it shall be the privilege of a Christian Scientist to confer with an M. D. on Ontology, or the Science of being.

Testimonials. SECT. 24. "Glorify God in your body, and in your spirit, which are God's" (St. Paul). Testimony in regard to the healing of the sick is highly important. More than a mere rehearsal of blessings, it scales the pinnacle of praise and illustrates the demonstration of Christ, "who healeth all thy diseases" (Psalm 103:3). This testimony, however, shall not include a description of symptoms or of suffering, though the generic name of the disease may be indicated. This By-Law applies to testimonials which appear in the periodicals and to those which are given at the Wednesday evening meeting.

Charity to All. SECT. 25. While members of this Church do not believe in the doctrines of theosophy, hypnotism, or spiritualism, they

1 cherish no enmity toward those who do believe
in such doctrines, and will not harm them. But
3 whenever God calls a member to bear testimony
to Truth and to defend the Cause of Christ, he
shall do it with love and without fear.

6 **Uncharitable Publications.** SECT. 26. A
member of this Church shall not publish, nor
cause to be published, an article that is unchari-
9 table or impertinent towards religion, medicine,
the courts, or the laws of our land.

The Golden Rule. SECT. 27. A member of
12 The Mother Church shall not haunt Mrs. Eddy's
drive when she goes out, continually stroll by
her house, or make a summer resort near her
15 for such a purpose.

Numbering the People. SECT. 28. Christian
Scientists shall not report for publication the
18 number of the members of The Mother Church,
nor that of the branch churches. According to
the Scripture they shall turn away from person-
21 ality and numbering the people.

Our Church Edifices. SECT. 29. The periodicals of our denomination do not publish de-
24 scriptions of our church edifices, but they may
quote from other periodicals or give incidental
narratives.

No Monopoly. SECT. 30.   A Scientist shall
not endeavor to monopolize the healing work in
any church or locality, to the exclusion of others,
but all who understand the teachings of Christian
Science are privileged to enter into this holy work,
and "by their fruits ye shall know them."

Christian Science Nurse. SECT. 31.   A member of The Mother Church who represents himself or herself as a Christian Science nurse shall
be one who has a demonstrable knowledge of
Christian Science practice, who thoroughly understands the practical wisdom necessary in a sick
room, and who can take proper care of the sick.

The cards of such persons may be inserted in
The Christian Science Journal under rules established by the publishers.

Article IX
MARRIAGE AND DECEASE

A Legal Ceremony. SECTION 1.   If a Christian Scientist is to be married, the ceremony
shall be performed by a clergyman who is legally
authorized.

Sudden Decease. SECT. 2.   If a member of
The Mother Church shall decease suddenly, without previous injury or illness, and the cause

1 thereof be unknown, an autopsy shall be made
by qualified experts. When it is possible the
3 body of a female shall be prepared for burial by
one of her own sex.

Article X
6   DEBATING IN PUBLIC

No Unauthorized Debating. SECTION 1. A
member of this Church shall not debate on Chris-
9 tian Science in public debating assemblies, without the consent of the Board of Directors.

Article XI
12   COMPLAINTS

Departure from Tenets. SECTION 1. If a
member of this Church shall depart from the
15 Tenets and be found having the name without
the life of a Christian Scientist, and another
member in good standing shall from Christian
18 motives make this evident, a meeting of the Board
of Directors shall be called, and the offender's
case shall be tried and said member exonerated,
21 put on probation, or excommunicated.

Violation of By-Laws. SECT. 2. A member
who is found violating any of the By-Laws

or Rules herein set forth, shall be admonished 1
in consonance with the Scriptural demand in
Matthew 18:15–17; and if he neglect to accept 3
such admonition, he shall be placed on probation,
or if he repeat the offense, his name shall be
dropped from the roll of Church membership. 6

Violation of Christian Fellowship.   SECT. 3.
Any member who shall unjustly aggrieve or
vilify the Pastor Emeritus or another member, 9
or who does not live in Christian fellowship with
members who are in good and regular standing
with this Church, shall either withdraw from the 12
Church or be excommunicated.

Preliminary Requirement.   SECT. 4.   No
Church discipline shall ensue until the require- 15
ments according to the Scriptures, in Matthew
18:15–17, have been strictly obeyed, unless a
By-Law governing the case provides for imme- 18
diate action.

Authority.   SECT. 5.   The Christian Science
Board of Directors has power to discipline, place 21
on probation, remove from membership, or to
excommunicate members of The Mother Church.
Only the members of this Board shall be pres- 24
ent at meetings for the examination of complaints against Church members; and they alone

¹ shall vote on cases involving The Mother Church
discipline.

³ **Members in Mother Church Only.** SECT. 6.
A complaint against a member of The Mother
Church, *if said member belongs to no branch*
⁶ *church* and if this complaint is not for *mental
malpractice,* shall be laid before this Board, and
within ten days thereafter, the Clerk of the
⁹ Church shall address a letter of inquiry to the
member complained of as to the validity of
the charge. If a member is found guilty of that
¹² whereof he is accused and his previous character
has been good, his confession of his error and
evidence of his compliance with our Church
¹⁵ Rules shall be deemed sufficient by the Board
for forgiveness for once, and the Clerk of the
Church shall immediately so inform him. But
¹⁸ a second offense shall dismiss a member from
the Church.

Working Against the Cause. SECT. 7. If a
²¹ member of this Church shall, mentally or otherwise, persist in working against the interests of
another member, or the interests of our Pastor
²⁴ Emeritus and the accomplishment of what she
understands is advantageous to this Church and
to the Cause of Christian Science, or shall influ-

ence others thus to act, upon her complaint or the complaint of a member for her or for himself, it shall be the duty of the Board of Directors immediately to call a meeting, and drop forever the name of the member guilty of this offense from the roll of Church membership.

No Unchristian Conduct. SECT. 8. If a member of this Church were to treat the author of our textbook disrespectfully and cruelly, upon her complaint that member should be excommunicated. If a member, without her having requested the information, shall trouble her on subjects unnecessarily and without her consent, it shall be considered an offense.

Not to Learn Hypnotism. SECT. 9. Members of this Church shall not learn hypnotism on penalty of being excommunicated from this Church. No member shall enter a complaint of mental malpractice for a sinister purpose. If the author of SCIENCE AND HEALTH shall bear witness to the offense of mental malpractice, it shall be considered a sufficient evidence thereof.

Publications Unjust. SECT. 10. If a member of The Mother Church publishes, or causes to be published, an article that is false or unjust, hence injurious, to Christian Science or to its

1 Leader, and if, upon complaint by another member, the Board of Directors finds that the offense
3 has been committed, the offender shall be suspended for not less than three years from his or her office in this Church and from Church
6 membership.

The Mother Church of Christ, Scientist, Tenets. SECT. 11. If a member of The Mother
9 Church of Christ, Scientist, or a member of a branch of this Church break the rules of its Tenets as to unjust and unmerciful conduct —
12 on complaint of Mrs. Eddy our Pastor Emeritus — and this complaint being found valid, his or her name shall be erased from The Mother
15 Church and the branch church's list of membership and the offender shall not be received into The Mother Church or a branch church
18 for twelve years.

Special Offense. SECT. 12. If a member of this Church, either by word or work, represents
21 falsely to or of the Leader and Pastor Emeritus, said member shall immediately be disciplined, and a second similar offense shall remove his or her
24 name from membership in The Mother Church.

Members of Branch Churches. SECT. 13. A member of both The Mother Church and a branch

Church of Christ, Scientist, or a Reader, shall not 1
report nor send notices to The Mother Church,
or to the Pastor Emeritus, of errors of the mem- 3
bers of their local church; but they shall strive
to overcome these errors.   Each church shall
separately and independently discipline its own 6
members, — if this sad necessity occurs.

Article XII

TEACHERS   9

Probation.   SECTION 1.   For sufficient reasons it may be decided that a teacher has so
strayed as not to be fit for the work of a Reader 12
in church or a teacher of Christian Science.
Although repentant and forgiven by the Church
and retaining his membership, this weak member 15
shall not be counted loyal till after three years
of exemplary character.   Then the Board of
Directors may decide if his loyalty has been 18
proved by uniform maintenance of the life of
a consistent, consecrated Christian Scientist.

Misteaching.   SECT. 2.   If a member of this 21
Church is found trying to practise or to teach
Christian Science contrary to the statement
thereof in its textbook, SCIENCE AND HEALTH 24

1 WITH KEY TO THE SCRIPTURES, it shall be the
duty of the Board of Directors to admonish
3 that member according to Article XI, Sect. 4.
Then, if said member persists in this offense,
his or her name shall be dropped from the roll
6 of this Church.

MEETINGS

Article XIII

9   REGULAR AND SPECIAL MEETINGS

Annual Meetings. SECTION 1. The regular
meetings of The Mother Church shall be held
12 annually, on Monday following the first Sunday
in June. No other than its officers are required
to be present. These assemblies shall be for
15 listening to the reports of Treasurer, Clerk, and
Committees, and general reports from the Field.
Meetings of Board of Directors. SECT. 2.
18 The annual meeting of the Christian Science
Board of Directors, for electing officers and
other business, shall be held on Monday preced-
21 ing the annual meeting of the Church. Regular
meetings for electing candidates to membership

with The Mother Church, and for the transac- 1
tion of such other business as may properly come
before these meetings, shall be held on the Fri- 3
day preceding the first Sunday in June, and on
the first Friday in November of each year. Special meetings may be held at any time upon the 6
call of the Clerk.

Called only by the Clerk. SECT. 3. Before
calling a meeting of the members of this Church 9
(excepting its regular sessions) it shall be the
duty of the Clerk to inform the Board of Directors and the Pastor Emeritus of his intention, 12
and to state definitely the purpose for which the
members are to convene. The Clerk must have
the consent of this Board and the Pastor Emer- 15
itus, before he can call said meeting.

CHURCH SERVICES

Article XIV
THE CHRISTIAN SCIENCE PASTOR

Ordination. SECTION 1.   I, Mary Baker
Eddy, ordain the BIBLE, and SCIENCE AND
HEALTH WITH KEY TO THE SCRIPTURES, Pastor
over The Mother Church, — The First Church
of Christ, Scientist, in Boston, Mass., — and
they will continue to preach for this Church
and the world.

The Lesson-Sermon. SECT. 2.   The subject
of the Lesson-Sermon in the morning service of
The Mother Church, and of the branch Churches
of Christ, Scientist, shall be repeated at the other
services on Sunday.   The correlative Biblical
texts in the Lesson-Sermon shall extend from
Genesis to Revelation.

Article XV
READING IN PUBLIC

Announcing Author's Name.   SECTION 1.
To pour into the ears of listeners the sacred

revelations of Christian Science indiscriminately, or without characterizing their origin and thus distinguishing them from the writings of authors who think at random on this subject, is to lose some weight in the scale of right thinking. Therefore it is the duty of every member of this Church, when publicly reading or quoting from the books or poems of our Pastor Emeritus, first to announce the name of the author. Members shall also instruct their pupils to adopt the aforenamed method for the benefit of our Cause.

Article XVI

WELCOMING STRANGERS

The Leader's Welcome. SECTION 1. Mrs. Eddy welcomes to her seats in the church, persons of all sects and denominations who come to listen to the Sunday sermon and are not otherwise provided with seats.

The Local Members' Welcome. SECT. 2. It shall be the duty and privilege of the local members of The Mother Church to give their seats, if necessary, to strangers who may come to attend the morning services.

Article XVII
SERVICES UNINTERRUPTED

Continued Throughout the Year. SECTION 1.
The services of The Mother Church shall be
continued twelve months each year. One meeting on Sunday during the months of July and
August is sufficient. A Christian Scientist is
not fatigued by prayer, by reading the Scriptures
or the Christian Science textbook. Amusement
or idleness is weariness. Truth and Love rest
the weary and heavy laden.

Easter Observances. SECT. 2. In the United
States there shall be no special observances,
festivities, nor gifts at the Easter season by
members of The Mother Church. Gratitude
and love should abide in every heart each day
of all the years. Those sacred words of our
beloved Master, "Let the dead bury their dead,"
and "Follow thou me," appeal to daily Christian
endeavors for the living whereby to exemplify
our risen Lord.

Laying a Corner Stone. SECT. 3. No large
gathering of people nor display shall be allowed
when laying the Corner Stone of a Church of
Christ, Scientist. Let the ceremony be devout.

No special trowel should be used. (See SCIENCE 1
AND HEALTH, page 140.)

Overflow Meetings. SECT. 4. A Church of 3
Christ, Scientist, shall not hold two or more
Sunday services at the same hour.

Article XVIII   6
COMMUNION

No more Communion. SECTION 1. The
Mother Church of Christ, Scientist, shall observe 9
no more Communion seasons.

Communion of Branch Churches. SECT. 2.
The Communion shall be observed in the branch 12
churches on the second Sunday in January and
July of each year, and at this service the Tenets
of The Mother Church are to be read.   15

Article XIX
MUSIC IN THE CHURCH

Soloist and Organist. SECTION 1. The music 18
in The Mother Church shall not be operatic, but
of an appropriate religious character and of a
recognized standard of musical excellence; it 21
shall be played in a dignified and suitable manner. Music from the organ alone should continue about eight or nine minutes for the 24

voluntary and six or seven minutes for the post-
lude, the offertory conforming to the time required to take the collection. The solo singer
shall not neglect to sing any special hymn selected
by the Board of Directors.

Article XX
SUNDAY SCHOOL

The Sunday School. SECTION 1. Pupils may
be received in the Sunday School classes of any
Church of Christ, Scientist, up to the age of
twenty years, and by transfer from another
Church of Christ, Scientist, up to that age, but
no pupil shall remain in the Sunday School of
any Church of Christ, Scientist, after reaching
the age of twenty. None except the officers,
teachers, and pupils should attend the Sunday
School exercises.

Teaching the Children. SECT. 2. The
Sabbath School children shall be taught the
Scriptures, and they shall be instructed according to their understanding or ability to grasp
the simpler meanings of the divine Principle that
they are taught.

Subject for Lessons. SECT. 3. The first
lessons of the children should be the Ten Com-

mandments (Exodus 20: 3-17), the Lord's
Prayer (Matt. 6: 9-13), and its Spiritual Interpretation by Mary Baker Eddy, Sermon on
the Mount (Matt. 5: 3-12). The next lessons consist of such questions and answers as
are adapted to a juvenile class, and may be
found in the Christian Science Quarterly Lessons,
read in Church services. The instruction given
by the children's teachers must not deviate from
the absolute Christian Science contained in their
textbook.

READING ROOMS

Article XXI

Establishment. SECTION 1. Each church of
the Christian Science denomination shall have
a Reading Room, though two or more churches
may unite in having Reading Rooms, provided
these rooms are well located.

Librarian. SECT. 2. The individuals who
take charge of the Reading Rooms of The
Mother Church shall be elected by the Christian
Science Board of Directors, subject to the approval of Mary Baker Eddy. He or she shall
have no bad habits, shall have had experience in

1 the Field, shall be well educated, and a devout
Christian Scientist.[1]

3 **Literature in Reading Rooms.** SECT. 3. The
literature sold or exhibited in the Reading Rooms
of Christian Science Churches shall consist only
6 of *Science and Health with Key to the Scrip-*
tures, by Mary Baker Eddy, and other writings
by this author; also the literature published or
9 sold by The Christian Science Publishing Society.

RELATION AND DUTIES OF MEMBERS
TO PASTOR EMERITUS

12   Article XXII

The Title of Mother Changed. SECTION 1.
In the year eighteen hundred and ninety-five,
15 loyal Christian Scientists had given to the author
of their textbook, the Founder of Christian Science, the individual, endearing term of Mother.
18 At first Mrs. Eddy objected to being called thus,
but afterward consented on the ground that this
appellative in the Church meant nothing more
21 than a tender term such as sister or brother. In
the year nineteen hundred and three and after,
owing to the public misunderstanding of this
24 name, it is the duty of Christian Scientists to

---
[1] See also Article XXV, Sect. 7.

drop the word *mother* and to substitute Leader, 1
already used in our periodicals.

A Member not a Leader.   SECT. 2.   A 3
member of The First Church of Christ, Scientist, in Boston, Mass., shall not be called
Leader by members of this Church, when this 6
term is used in connection with Christian
Science.

Obedience Required.   SECT. 3.   It shall be 9
the duty of the officers of this Church, of the
editors of the *Christian Science Journal, Sentinel,* and *Der Heròld,* of the members of the 12
Committees on Publication, of the Trustees of
The Christian Science Publishing Society, and
of the Board of Education promptly to comply 15
with any written order, signed by Mary Baker
Eddy, which applies to their official functions.
Disobedience to this By-Law shall be sufficient 18
cause for the removal of the offending member
from office.

The vacancy shall be supplied by a majority 21
vote of the Christian Science Board of Directors, and the candidate shall be subject to the
approval of Mary Baker Eddy.   24

Understanding Communications.   SECT. 4.
If the Clerk of this Church shall receive a com-

1 munication from the Pastor Emeritus which he
does not fully understand, he shall inform her
3 of this fact before presenting it to the Church
and obtain a clear understanding of the matter,
— then act in accordance therewith.

6 **Interpreting Communications.**   SECT. 5.   If
at a meeting of this Church a doubt or dis-
agreement shall arise among the members as to
9 the signification of the communications of the
Pastor Emeritus to them, before action is taken
it shall be the duty of the Clerk to report to her
12 the vexed question and to await her explanation
thereof.

Reading and Attesting Letters.   SECT. 6.
15 When a letter or a message from the Pastor
Emeritus is brought before a meeting of this
Church, or she is referred to as authority for
18 business, it shall be the duty of the Church to
inquire if all of the letter has been read, and to
require all of it to be read;   also to have any
21 authority supposed to come from her satisfactorily attested.

Unauthorized Reports.   SECT. 7.   Members
24 of this Church shall not report on authority an
order from Mrs. Eddy that she has not sent,
either to the Boards or to the executive bodies

of this Church. The Pastor Emeritus is not to
be consulted on cases of discipline, on the cases
of candidates for admission to this Church, or
on the cases of those on trial for dismissal from
the Church.

Private Communications. SECT. 8. A strictly
private communication from the Pastor Emeritus
to a member of her Church shall not be made
public without her written consent.

Unauthorized Legal Action. SECT. 9. A
member of this Church shall not employ an at-
torney, nor take legal action on a case not provided for in its By-Laws — if said case relates
to the person or to the property of Mary Baker
Eddy — without having personally conferred
with her on said subject.

Duty to God. SECT. 10. Members of this
Church who turn their attention from the divine
Principle of being to personality, sending gifts,
congratulatory despatches or letters to the Pastor
Emeritus on Thanksgiving, Christmas, New Year,
or Easter, break a rule of this Church and are
amenable therefor.

Opportunity for Serving the Leader. SECT.
11. At the written request of the Pastor Emeritus, Mrs. Eddy, the Board of Directors shall

1 immediately notify a person who has been a
member of this Church at least three years to
3 go in ten days to her, and it shall be the duty
of the member thus notified to remain with Mrs.
Eddy three years consecutively. A member who
6 leaves her in less time without the Directors'
consent or who declines to obey this call to
duty, upon Mrs. Eddy's complaint thereof shall
9 be excommunicated from The Mother Church.
Members thus serving the Leader shall be paid
semi-annually at the rate of one thousand dol-
12 lars yearly in addition to rent and board. Those
members whom she teaches the course in Divin-
ity, and who remain with her three consecutive
15 years, receive the degree of the Massachusetts
Metaphysical College.

Location. SECT. 12. Rev. Mary Baker Eddy
18 calls to her home or allows to visit or to locate
therein only those individuals whom she engages
through the Christian Science Board of Direc-
21 tors of The Mother Church. This By-Law takes
effect on Dec. 15, 1908.

Agreement Required. SECT. 13. When the
24 Christian Science Board of Directors calls a student in accordance with Article XXII, Sect. 11,
of our Church Manual to the home of their

Leader, Mrs. Eddy, said student shall come under
a signed agreement to remain with Mrs. Eddy
if she so desires, during the time specified in the
Church Manual.

Incomplete Term of Service. SECT. 14. If a
student who has been called to serve our Leader
in accordance with Article XXII, Sect. 11, of
the Church Manual leaves her before the expiration of the time therein mentioned such student
shall pay to Mrs. Eddy whatsoever she may
charge for what she has taught him or her during the time of such service.

Help. SECT. 15. If the author of the Christian Science textbook call on this Board for
household help or a handmaid, the Board shall
immediately appoint a proper member of this
Church therefor, and the appointee shall go immediately in obedience to the call. "He that lov-
eth father or mother more than me is not worthy
of me." (Matt. 10:37.)

Students with Mrs. Eddy. SECT. 16. Students employed by Mrs. Eddy at her home shall
not take care of their churches or attend to other
affairs outside of her house.

Mrs. Eddy's Room. SECT. 17. The room in
The Mother Church formerly known as "Mother's
Room" shall hereafter be closed to visitors.

Pastor Emeritus to be Consulted. SECT. 18. The Mother Church shall not make a church By-Law, nor enter into a business transaction with a Christian Scientist in the employ of Rev. Mary Baker Eddy, without first consulting her on said subject and adhering strictly to her advice thereon.

THE MOTHER CHURCH AND BRANCH CHURCHES

Article XXIII

Local Self-government. SECTION 1. The Mother Church of Christ, Scientist, shall assume no general official control of other churches, and it shall be controlled by none other.

Each Church of Christ, Scientist, shall have its own form of government. No conference of churches shall be held, unless it be when our churches, located in the same State, convene to confer on a statute of said State, or to confer harmoniously on individual unity and action of the churches in said State.

Titles. SECT. 2. "The First Church of Christ, Scientist," is the legal title of The Mother

Church. Branch churches of The Mother Church may take the title of First Church of Christ, Scientist; Second Church of Christ, Scientist; and so on, where more than one church is established in the same place; but the article "The" must not be used before titles of branch churches, nor written on applications for membership in naming such churches.

Mother Church Unique. SECT. 3. In its relation to other Christian Science churches, in its By-Laws and self-government, The Mother Church stands alone; it occupies a position that no other church can fill. Then for a branch church to assume such position would be disastrous to Christian Science. Therefore, no Church of Christ, Scientist, shall be considered loyal that has branch churches or adopts The Mother Church's form of government, except in such cases as are specially allowed and named in this Manual.

Tenets Copyrighted. SECT. 4. Branch churches shall not write the Tenets of The Mother Church in their church books, except they give the name of their author and her permission to publish them as Tenets of The Mother Church, copyrighted in SCIENCE AND HEALTH WITH KEY TO THE SCRIPTURES.

1   **Manual.**   SECT. 5.   Branch churches shall
not adopt, print, nor publish the Manual of The
3 Mother Church. See Article XXXV, Sect. 1.

Organizing Churches. SECT. 6.   A member
of this Church who obeys its By-Laws and is a
6 loyal exemplary Christian Scientist working in
the Field, is eligible to form a church in con-
formity with Sect. 7 of this Article, and to
9 have church services conducted by reading the
SCRIPTURES and the Christian Science textbook.
This church shall be acknowledged publicly as a
12 Church of Christ, Scientist. Upon proper application, made in accordance with the rules of The
Christian Science Publishing Society, the serv-
15 ices of such a church may be advertised in *The
Christian Science Journal.* The branch churches
shall be individual, and not more than two small
18 churches shall consolidate under one church government.   If the Pastor Emeritus, Mrs. Eddy,
should relinquish her place as the head or Leader
21 of The Mother Church of Christ, Scientist, each
branch church shall continue its present form of
government in consonance with The Mother
24 Church Manual.

**Requirements   for   Organizing   Branch
Churches.** SECT. 7.   A branch church of The
27 First Church of Christ, Scientist, Boston, Mass.,

shall not be organized with less than sixteen loyal
Christian Scientists, four of whom are members
of The Mother Church. This membership shall
include at least one active practitioner whose card
is published in the list of practitioners in *The
Christian Science Journal.*

Privilege of Members. SECT. 8. Members
in good standing with The Mother Church, who
are members of the faculty, instructors, or students in any university or college, can form and
conduct a Christian Science organization at such
university or college, provided its rules so permit.
Also members in good standing with The Mother
Church, who are graduates of said university
or college, may become members of the organization by application to, and by the unanimous
vote of, the active members present, if the rules
of the university or college so permit. When
called for, a member of the Board of Lectureship may lecture for said university or college
organization.

No Close Communion. SECT. 9. The
Mother Church and the branch churches shall
not confine their membership to the pupils of
one teacher.

No Interference. SECT. 10. A member of The
Mother Church may be a member of one branch

Church of Christ, Scientist, or of one Christian Science society holding public services, but he shall not be a member of both a branch church and a society; neither shall he exercise supervision or control over any other church. In Christian Science each branch church shall be distinctly democratic in its government, and no individual, and no other church shall interfere with its affairs.

Teachers' and Practitioners' Offices. SECT. 11. Teachers and practitioners of Christian Science shall not have their offices or rooms in the branch churches, in the Reading Rooms, nor in rooms connected therewith.

Recognition. SECT. 12. In order to be eligible to a card in *The Christian Science Journal,* churches and societies are required to acknowledge as such all other Christian Science churches and societies advertised in said *Journal,* and to maintain toward them an attitude of Christian fellowship.

GUARDIANSHIP OF CHURCH FUNDS   1

Article XXIV

Church Edifice a Testimonial. SECTION 1. 3
Whereas, on March 20, 1895, the Christian Science Board of Directors, in behalf of The First Church of Christ, Scientist, Boston, Mass., 6
presented to Rev. Mary Baker Eddy their church edifice as a Testimonial of this Church's love and gratitude, and she, with grateful ac- 9
knowledgments thereof, declined to receive this munificent gift, she now understands the financial situation between the Christian Science 12
Board of Directors and said Church to be as follows: —

Financial Situation. SECT. 2. The Christian 15
Science Board of Directors owns the church edifices, with the land whereon they stand, legally; and the Church members own the aforesaid 18
premises and buildings, beneficially. After the first church was built, the balance of the building funds, which remained in the hands of the 21
Directors, belonged to the Church, and not solely to the Directors. The balance of the church

building funds, which can be spared after the debts are paid, should remain on safe deposit, to be hereafter used for the benefit of this Church, as the right occasion may call for it. The following indicates the proper management of the Church funds: —

Report of Directors. SECT. 3. It shall be the duty of the Christian Science Board of Directors to have the books of the Church Treasurer audited semi-annually, and to report at the annual Church meeting the amount of funds which the Church has on hand, the amount of its indebtedness and of its expenditures for the last year.

Finance Committee. SECT. 4. There shall be a Committee on Finance, which shall consist of three members of this Church in good standing. Its members shall be appointed annually by the Christian Science Board of Directors and with the consent of the Pastor Emeritus. They shall hold quarterly meetings and keep themselves thoroughly informed as to the real estate owned by this Church and the amount of funds received by the Treasurer of The Mother Church, who is individually responsible for said funds. They shall have the books of the Christian Science

Board of Directors and the books of the Church
Treasurer audited annually by an honest, competent accountant. The books are to be audited
on May first.

Prior to paying bills against the Church, the
Treasurer of this Church shall submit them all
to said committee for examination. This committee shall decide thereupon by a unanimous
vote, and its endorsement of the bills shall render
them payable.

If it be found that the Church funds have not
been properly managed, it shall be the duty of
the Board of Directors and the Treasurer to be
individually responsible for the performance of
their several offices satisfactorily, and for the
proper distribution of the funds of which they
are the custodians.

God's Requirement. SECT. 5. God requires
wisdom, economy, and brotherly love to characterize all the proceedings of the members of
The Mother Church, The First Church of Christ,
Scientist.

Provision for the Future. SECT. 6. In case
of any possible future deviation from duty, the
Committee on Finance shall visit the Board of
Directors, and, in a Christian spirit and manner,

demand that each member thereof comply with the By-Laws of the Church. If any Director fails to heed this admonition, he may be dismissed from office and the vacancy supplied by the Board.

Debt and Duty. SECT. 7. The Mother Church shall not be made legally responsible for the debts of individuals except such debts as are specified in its By-Laws. Donations from this Church shall not be made without the written consent of the Pastor Emeritus. Also important movements of the manager of the Committee on Publication shall be sanctioned by the Board of Directors and be subject to the approval of Mary Baker Eddy. (See Article I, Sect. 6.)

Emergencies. SECT. 8. The Treasurer, personally, or through the Clerk of the Church, may pay from the funds of the Church bills of immediate necessity not exceeding $200 for any one transaction, and he may keep on deposit the sum of $500 with the Clerk, as a petty cash fund, to be used by him for the payment of such bills. Such payments shall be reported, on the first of the following month, to the Board of Directors and the Committee on Finance, for their approval.

Committee on Business. SECT. 9. The Christian Science Board of Directors shall elect annually a Committee on Business, which shall consist of not less than three loyal members of The Mother Church, who shall transact promptly and efficiently such business as Mrs. Eddy, the Directors, or the Committee on Publication shall commit to it. While the members of this Committee are engaged in the transaction of the business assigned to them they shall be paid from the Church funds. Before being eligible for office the names of the persons nominated for said office shall be presented to Mrs. Eddy for her written approval.

THE CHRISTIAN SCIENCE PUBLISHING SOCIETY

Article XXV

Board of Trustees. SECTION 1. The Board of Trustees, constituted by a Deed of Trust given by Rev. Mary Baker Eddy, the Pastor Emeritus of this Church, on January twenty-fifth, 1898, shall hold and manage the property therein conveyed, and conduct the business of

1 "The Christian Science Publishing Society" on
a strictly Christian basis, for the promotion of
3 the interests of Christian Science.

Disposal of Funds. SECT. 2. The net profits
of the business shall be paid over semi-annually
6 to the Treasurer of The Mother Church. He
shall hold this money subject to the order of
the Christian Science Board of Directors, which
9 is authorized to order its disposition only in
accordance with the By-Laws contained in this
Manual.

12 **Vacancies in Trusteeship.** SECT. 3. The
Christian Science Board of Directors shall have
the power to declare vacancies in said trusteeship,
15 for such reasons as to the Board may seem ex-
pedient.

Whenever a vacancy shall occur, the Pastor
18 Emeritus reserves the right to fill the same by
appointment; but if she does not elect to exercise this right, the remaining trustees shall fill
21 the vacancy, subject to her approval.

Editors and Manager. SECT. 4. The term
of office for the editors and the manager of The
24 Christian Science Publishing Society is one year
each, dating from the time of election to the
office. Incumbents who have served one year or

more can be re-elected, or new officers elected, by a unanimous vote of the Christian Science Board of Directors, and the consent of the Pastor Emeritus given in her own handwriting.

Suitable Employees. SECT. 5. A person who is not accepted by the Pastor Emeritus and the Christian Science Board of Directors as suitable, shall in no manner be connected with publishing her books, nor with editing or publishing *The Christian Science Journal, Christian Science Sentinel, Der Herold der Christian Science,* nor with The Christian Science Publishing Society.

Periodicals. SECT. 6. Periodicals which shall at any time be published by The Christian Science Publishing Society, shall be copyrighted and conducted according to the provisions in the Deed of Trust relating to *The Christian Science Journal.*

Rule of Conduct. SECT. 7. No objectionable pictures shall be exhibited in the rooms where the Christian Science textbook is published or sold. No idle gossip, no slander, no mischief-making, no evil speaking shall be allowed.

Books to be Published. SECT. 8. Only the Publishing Society of The Mother Church selects, approves, and publishes the books and literature it sends forth. If Mary Baker Eddy disapproves of certain books or literature, the Society will not publish them. The Committees on Publication are in no manner connected with these functions. A book or an article of which Mrs. Eddy is the author shall not be published nor republished by this Society without her knowledge or written consent.

Removal of Cards. SECT. 9. No cards shall be removed from our periodicals without the request of the advertiser, except by a majority vote of the Christian Science Board of Directors at a meeting held for this purpose or for the examination of complaints.

Members of this Church who practise other professions or pursue other vocations, shall not advertise as healers, excepting those members who are officially engaged in the work of Christian Science, and they must devote ample time for faithful practice.

TEACHING CHRISTIAN SCIENCE   1

Article XXVI
TEACHERS   3

Motive in Teaching. SECTION 1. Teaching
Christian Science shall not be a question of
money, but of morals and religion, healing and   6
uplifting the race.

Care of Pupils. SECT. 2. Christian Scientists
who are teachers shall carefully select for pupils   9
such only as have good past records and promis-
ing proclivities toward Christian Science.   A
teacher shall not assume personal control of, or 12
attempt to dominate his pupils, but he shall hold
himself morally obligated to promote their progress in the understanding of divine Principle, not 15
only during the class term but after it, and to
watch well that they prove sound in sentiment
and practical in Christian Science. He shall per- 18
sistently and patiently counsel his pupils in con-
formity with the unerring laws of God, and shall
enjoin them habitually to study the Scriptures 21
and SCIENCE AND HEALTH WITH KEY TO THE
SCRIPTURES as a help thereto.

Defense against Malpractice. SECT. 3. Teachers shall instruct their pupils how to defend themselves against mental malpractice, never to return evil for evil, but to know the truth that makes free, and thus to be a law, not unto others, but to themselves.

Number of Pupils. SECT. 4. The teachers of Christian Science shall teach but one class yearly, which class shall consist of not more than thirty pupils. After 1907, the Board of Education shall have one class triennially, a Normal class not exceeding thirty pupils.

Pupil's Tuition. SECT. 5. A student's price for teaching Christian Science shall not exceed $100.00 per pupil.

Associations. SECT. 6. The associations of the pupils of loyal teachers shall convene annually. The pupils shall be guided by the BIBLE, and SCIENCE AND HEALTH, not by their teachers' personal views. Teachers shall not call their pupils together, or assemble a selected number of them, for more frequent meetings.

A Single Field of Labor. SECT. 7. A loyal teacher of Christian Science shall not teach another loyal teacher's pupil, except it be in the Board of Education. Outside of this Board each

student occupies only his own field of labor. 1
Pupils may visit each other's churches, and by
invitation attend each other's associations.   3

Caring for Pupils of Strayed Members.
SECT. 8.   A loyal teacher of Christian Science
may teach and receive into his association the 6
pupils of another member of this Church who
has so strayed as justly to be deemed, under the
provisions of Article XII, Sect. 1, not ready to 9
lead his pupils.

Teachers must have Certificates.   SECT. 9.
A member of this Church shall not teach pupils 12
Christian Science unless he has a certificate to
show that he has been taught by Mrs. Eddy or
has taken a Normal Course at the Massachu- 15
setts Metaphysical College or in the Board of
Education.

Such members who have not been continu- 18
ously active and loyal Christian Scientists since
receiving instruction as above, shall not teach
Christian Science without the approval of The 21
Christian Science Board of Directors.

Article XXVII
PUPILS

Authorized to Teach.   SECTION 1.   After a student's pupil has been duly authorized to be a teacher of Christian Science, or has been under the personal instruction of Mrs. Eddy, he is no longer under the jurisdiction of his former teacher.

Without Teachers.   SECT. 2.   Those beloved brethren whose teacher has left them, can elect an experienced Christian Scientist, who is not in charge of an association of students and who is ready for this high calling, to conduct the meetings of their association.

Basis for Teaching.   SECT. 3.   The teachers of the Normal class shall teach from the chapter "Recapitulation" in SCIENCE AND HEALTH WITH KEY TO THE SCRIPTURES, and from the Christian Science Platform, beginning on page 330 of the revised editions since 1902, and they shall teach nothing contrary thereto.   The teachers of the Primary class shall instruct their pupils from the said chapter on "Recapitulation" only.

Church Membership. SECT. 4. Neither the
Pastor Emeritus nor a member of this Church
shall teach Roman Catholics Christian Science,
except it be with the written consent of the
authority of their Church. Choice of patients is
left to the wisdom of the practitioner, and Mrs.
Eddy is not to be consulted on this subject.

Class Teaching. SECT. 5. Members of The
Mother Church who are authorized by its By-
Laws to teach Christian Science, shall not solicit,
or cause or permit others to solicit, pupils for their
classes. No member of this Church shall advise
against class instruction.

Teachers of Christian Science must have the
necessary moral and spiritual qualifications to
elucidate the Principle and rule of Christian Science, through the higher meaning of the Scriptures. "The less the teacher personally controls
other minds, and the more he trusts them to the
divine Truth and Love, the better it will be for
both teacher and student." (Retrospection and
Introspection, page 84.)

BOARD OF EDUCATION

Article XXVIII

ORGANIZATION

Officers. SECTION 1. There shall be a Board of Education, under the auspices of Mary Baker Eddy, President of the Massachusetts Metaphysical College, consisting of three members, a president, vice-president, and teacher of Christian Science. Obstetrics will not be taught.

Election. SECT. 2. The vice-president shall be elected annually by the Christian Science Board of Directors. Beginning with 1907, the teacher shall be elected every third year by said Board, and the candidate shall be subject to the approval of the Pastor Emeritus.

President not to be Consulted. SECT. 3. The President is not to be consulted by students on the question of applying for admission to this Board nor on their course or conduct. The students can confer with their teachers on subjects essential to their progress.

Presidency of College. SECT. 4. Should the President resign over her own signature or vacate her office of President of the Massachusetts Metaphysical College, a meeting of the Christian Science Board of Directors shall immediately be called, and the vice-president of the Board of Education being found worthy, on receiving her approval shall be elected to fill the vacancy.

Article XXIX
APPLICANTS AND GRADUATES

Normal Teachers. SECTION 1. Loyal students who have been taught in a Primary class by Mrs. Eddy and have practised Christian Science healing acceptably three years, and who present such credentials as are required to verify this fact, are eligible to receive the degree of C.S.D.

Qualifications. SECT. 2. Loyal Christian Scientists' pupils who so desire may apply to the Board of Education for instruction; and if they have practised Christian Science healing successfully three years and will furnish evidence of their eligibility therefor, they are eligible to enter the Normal class. All members of this class must be thorough English scholars.

Certificates. SECT. 3. Students are examined and given certificates by this Board if found qualified to receive them.

Article XXX

ACTION OF THE BOARD

Sessions. SECTION 1. The term of the Massachusetts Metaphysical College will open with the Board of Education on the first Wednesday of December. The sessions will continue not over one week. None but the teacher and members of the College class shall be present at the sessions, and no Primary classes shall be taught under the auspices of this Board.

Special Instruction. SECT. 2. Not less than two thorough lessons by a well qualified teacher shall be given to each Normal class on the subject of mental practice and *malpractice*. One student in the class shall prepare a paper on said subject that shall be read to the class, thoroughly discussed, and understood; this paper shall be given to the teacher, and he shall not allow it or a copy of it to remain, but shall destroy this paper.

Signatures. SECT. 3. The signature of the teacher and of the President of the College shall be on all certificates issued.

Remuneration and Free Scholarship. SECT. 4. Tuition of class instruction in the Board of Education shall be $100.00. The bearer of a card of free scholarship from the President, Rev. Mary Baker Eddy, shall be entitled to a free course in this department on presentation of the card to the teacher. Only the President gives free admission to classes.

Surplus Funds. SECT. 5. Any surplus funds left in the hands of the Board of Education shall be paid over annually to the Treasurer of The Mother Church.

Primary Students. SECT. 6. Students of Christian Science, duly instructed therein and with good moral records, not having the certificate of C.S.D. may enter the Normal class in the Board of Education, which will be held once in three years beginning A. D. 1907; provided their diplomas are for three *consecutive* years under Mrs. Eddy's daily conversation on Chris-

tian Science, or from the Massachusetts Metaphysical College Board of Education.

Healing Better than Teaching.   SECT. 7.
Healing the sick and the sinner with Truth dem-
onstrates what we affirm of Christian Science,
and nothing can substitute this demonstration.
I recommend that each member of this Church
shall strive to demonstrate by his or her practice,
that Christian Science heals the sick quickly and
wholly, thus proving this Science to be all that
we claim for it.

If both husband and wife are found duly qualified to teach Christian Science, either one, not
both, should teach yearly one class.

Not Members of The Mother Church.   SECT. 8.
No person shall receive instructions in Chris-
tian Science in any class in the Massachusetts
Metaphysical College, nor receive the degree of
C.S.B. or C.S.D., who is not a member of The
First Church of Christ, Scientist, in Boston,
Mass.

Only those persons who are members of this
Church and possessed of the qualifications named
in Sect. 9 of Article XXVI of these By-Laws
shall be deemed loyal teachers of Christian
Science.

BOARD OF LECTURESHIP

Article XXXI

ORGANIZATION AND DUTIES

Election. SECTION 1. This Church shall maintain a Board of Lectureship, the members of which shall be elected annually on Monday preceding the Annual Meeting, subject to the approval of the Pastor Emeritus. The lecture year shall begin July 1 of each year.

Duty of Lecturers. SECT. 2. It is the duty of the Board of Lectureship to include in each lecture a true and just reply to public topics condemning Christian Science, and to bear testimony to the facts pertaining to the life of the Pastor Emeritus. Each member shall mail to the Clerk of this Church copies of his lectures before delivering them.

No Disruption of Branch Churches. SECT. 3. The Board of Lectureship is not allowed in anywise to meddle with nor to disrupt the organization of branch churches. The lecturer can invite churches within the city whither he is called to unite in their attendance on his lecture, and so make for their churches a less lecture fee; but the churches shall decide their action.

Receptions.   SECT. 4.   As a rule there should be no receptions nor festivities after a lecture on Christian Science, but there may occur exceptions. If there be an individual who goes to hear and deride truth, he should go away contemplating truth; and he who goes to seek truth should have the opportunity to depart in quiet *thought* on that subject.

Circuit Lecturer.   SECT. 5.   Upon the written request of Mrs. Eddy, The Mother Church shall appoint a Circuit Lecturer. His term of office, if approved, shall not be less than three years. He shall lecture in the United States, in Canada, in Great Britain and Ireland.

A member shall neither resign nor transfer this sacred office.

Article XXXII
CALLS FOR LECTURES

From the Directors. SECTION 1. When the need is apparent, the Christian Science Board of Directors of The Mother Church may call on any member of this Board of Lectureship to lecture at such places and at such times as the cause of Christian Science demands.

From Branch Churches. SECT. 2. The branch Churches of Christ, Scientist, may apply through their clerks to a member of this Board of Lectureship for a speaker, and one shall be assigned them by the Board.

From Societies. SECT. 3. If called for, a member of the Board may lecture for a Society.

Annual Lectures. SECT. 4. The Mother Church and the branch churches shall call on the Board of Lectureship annually for one or more lectures.

No Lectures by Readers. SECT. 5. No lecture shall be given by a Reader during his term of Readership. The duties alone of a Reader are ample.

No Wednesday Evening Lectures. SECT. 6. The Board of Lectureship shall not appoint a lecture for Wednesday evening.

Lecture Fee. SECT. 7. The lecture fee shall be left to the discretion of the lecturer.

Expenses. SECT. 8. The lecturer's traveling expenses and the cost of hall shall be paid by the church that employs him.

Exceptional Cases. SECT. 9. If a lecturer receive a call to lecture in a place where he sees there is special need, and the local church is unable to meet the expense, he is at liberty to supply that need and trust to contributions for his fee.

COMMITTEE ON PUBLICATION

Article XXXIII

In The Mother Church. SECTION 1. There shall be appointed by The Mother Church a Committee on Publication, which shall consist of one loyal Christian Scientist who lives in Boston, and he shall be manager of the Committees on Publication throughout the United States, Canada, Great Britain and Ireland. He shall be elected annually by a unanimous vote of the Christian Science Board of Directors and the consent of the Pastor Emeritus given in her own handwriting, and shall receive an annual salary, paid quarterly, of not less than four thousand dollars.

Duties. SECT. 2. It shall be the duty of the Committee on Publication to correct in a Christian manner impositions on the public in regard to Christian Science, injustices done Mrs. Eddy or members of this Church by the daily press, by periodicals or circulated literature of any sort.

1 This Committee on Publication shall be responsible for correcting or having corrected a false
3 newspaper article which has not been replied to
by other Scientists, or which has been forwarded
to this Committee for the purpose of having him
6 reply to it. If the correction by the Committee
on Publication is not promptly published by the
periodical in which it is desirable that this cor-
9 rection shall appear, this Committee shall immediately apply for aid to the Committee on
Business. Furthermore, the Committee on Pub-
12 lication shall read the *last proof sheet* of such
an article and see that it is published according
to copy; he shall circulate in large quantities
15 the papers containing such an article, sending a
copy to the Clerk of the Church. It shall also
be the duty of the Committee on Publication to
18 have published each year in a leading Boston
newspaper the letter sent to the Pastor Emeritus
by the Church members in annual meeting as-
21 sembled. The State Committees on Publication
act under the direction of this Committee on
Publication.

24   **In Branch Churches.**   SECT. 3.   The Readers
of the three largest branch churches in each State
of the United States and in Canada shall annually

and alternately appoint a Committee on Publication to serve in their localities. For the purposes of this By-Law, the State of California shall
be considered as though it were two States, the
dividing line being the 36th parallel of latitude.
Each county of Great Britain and Ireland, except
as hereinafter specified, through the Readers of
its three largest branch churches, shall annually
and alternately appoint a Committee on Publication to serve in its locality. Each church is not
necessarily confined to its own members in select-
ing this Committee, but if preferred, can appoint
a Committee on Publication who is in good fellowship with another Church of Christ, Scientist.

This By-Law applies to all States except Massachusetts, in which the Committee on Publication is elected only by the Christian Science Board
of Directors. The Committee for the counties
in which London, England, is situated shall be
appointed by the Christian Science Board of
Directors, and he shall, in addition to his other
duties, act as District Manager of the Committees
on Publication for Great Britain and Ireland.

Appointment. SECT. 4. The Committees on
Publication shall consist of men generally. Each
State Committee shall be appointed by the First
and Second Readers of the church employing

said Committee. If prior to the meeting of the church for the election of officers, Mrs. Eddy shall send to the First Reader of the church the name of a candidate for its Committee on Publication, the Readers shall appoint said candidate. Or if she shall send a special request to any Committee on Publication, the request shall be carried out according to her directions.

Removal from Office. SECT. 5. If the Committee on Publication neglects to fulfil the obligations of his office according to these By-Laws, and this becomes apparent to the Christian Science Board of Directors, it shall be the duty of the Directors immediately to act upon this important matter in accordance with said By-Laws.

The Christian Science Board of Directors may notify any Church of Christ, Scientist, to remove its Committee on Publication and to appoint another Committee to fill the vacancy; and it shall be the duty of that church to comply with this request. In such cases it shall be the privilege of this Board to name the Committee if it so desires, and any Committee so named by the Board shall be elected by the branch church.

Case of Necessity. SECT. 6. If a suitable man is not obtainable for Committee on Publication, a suitable woman shall be elected. If at

any time the Christian Science Board of Direc- 1
tors shall determine that the manager of the
general Committee on Publication needs an as- 3
sistant, the Board shall, with the approval of the
Pastor Emeritus, appoint an assistant manager,
who shall receive an adequate salary from The 6
Mother Church.

CHURCH-BUILDING

Article XXXIV

Building Committee.   SECTION 1.   There shall be a Building Committee consisting of not less than three members, and this committee shall not be dissolved until the new church edifice is completed. This committee shall elect, dismiss, or supply a vacancy of its members by a majority vote.

Designation of Deeds.   SECT. 2.   All deeds of further purchases of land for The First Church of Christ, Scientist, in Boston, Mass., shall have named in them all the trusts mentioned in the deeds given by Albert Metcalf and E. Noyes Whitcomb in March, 1903; but this rule shall not apply to land purchased for any purpose other than the erection of a church edifice. Also there shall be incorporated in all such deeds the phrase, "Mary Baker Eddy's Church, The

Mother Church or The First Church of Christ,
Scientist, in Boston, Mass."

The Mother Church Building. SECT. 3. The
edifice erected in 1894 for The First Church of
Christ, Scientist, in Boston, Mass., shall neither
be demolished, nor removed from the site where
it was built, without the written consent of the
Pastor Emeritus, Mary Baker Eddy.

CHURCH MANUAL

Article XXXV

For The Mother Church Only. SECTION 1.
The Church Manual of The First Church of
Christ, Scientist, in Boston, Mass., written by
Mary Baker Eddy and copyrighted, is adapted
to The Mother Church only. It stands alone,
uniquely adapted to form the budding thought
and hedge it about with divine Love. This
Manual shall not be revised without the written
consent of its author.

Seventy-third Edition the Authority. SECT. 2.
The Board of Directors, the Committee on Bible
Lessons, and the Board of Trustees shall each
keep a copy of the Seventy-third Edition and of
subsequent editions of the Church Manual; and
if a discrepancy appears in any revised edition,
these editions shall be cited as authority.

Amendment of By-Laws.   SECT. 3.   No new
Tenet or By-Law shall be adopted, nor any
Tenet or By-Law amended or annulled, without the written consent of Mary Baker Eddy, the
author of our textbook, SCIENCE AND HEALTH.

Appendix

Appendix

**Special Instructions
Regarding Applications for Church Membership**

1. Loyal members of The Mother Church are eligible to approve candidates to unite with this Church.

2. No persons are eligible to countersign applications except loyal students of Mrs. Eddy, Directors, and students of the Board of Education who have been given a degree, and are members of The Mother Church.

3. Those who approve applicants should have applications returned to them after being filled out by the applicants, as required by Article V, Sect. 6, and should compare them with the forms here given, and see that names are legibly written, before sending them to the Clerk of the Church. If not correct, the applicant will be notified, and new applications will

109

1 be required, as none will be returned that are
not correctly made out. This requirement is to
3 prevent applications being duplicated and the
confusion that might result therefrom. It is
important that these seemingly strict conditions
6 be exactly complied with, as the names of the
members of The Mother Church will be recorded
in the history of the Church and become a part
9 thereof.

4. All names, whether of applicants, ap-
provers, or countersigners, must be plainly
12 written, and one, at least, of the given names of
each, written in full. Initials only of first names
will not be received. Women must sign "Miss"
15 or "Mrs." before their names as the case may be.

All names must be written the same in all
places where they are required.

TO APPLICANTS   1

1.   In filling out the application blank, one
of the Christian names must be written in full.   3
Initials alone will not be received.

2.   If the applicant is a married woman she
must sign her own Christian name, not her hus-   6
band's, and prefix her signature with "Mrs;"
unmarried women must sign "Miss."

3.   There are two regular forms of applica-   9
tion.   1. For those who have studied Christian
Science with an authorized teacher; 2. For those
who have not studied Christian Science with a   12
teacher.

Applicants will find the chief points of these
instructions illustrated in Form 1 and Form 2,   15
on pages 114 and 118.

4.   Those whose teachers are deceased, absent,
or disloyal, or those whose teachers refuse, with-   18
out sufficient cause, to sign applications (see
Art. V, Sect. 4), will be furnished special forms
on application to the Clerk.   21

5. When branch churches are designated by number, as First Church, Second Church, etc., the number must be written First, Second, as shown on page 118. The article "the" either capitalized (The), or small (the), must not be used before titles of branch churches. See Article XXIII, Sect. 2.

6. If the applicant is not a member of a branch church, he should fill out his application in this respect according to the form on page 114.

Application Forms

Application I

PROPERLY SIGNED AND ENDORSED, ACCORDING TO ARTICLE V, SECT. 2

FORM 1.

The First Church of Christ, Scientist, in Boston, Mass., is designed to be built on the rock of Christ — Truth and Life — and to reflect the Church Triumphant.

One who is not a member of any church, excepting a branch church of Christ, Scientist, who loves Christian Science, and reads understandingly the Bible, and SCIENCE AND HEALTH WITH KEY TO THE SCRIPTURES, by Reverend Mary Baker Eddy, and other works by this author, and who is Christianly qualified and can enter into full fellowship with the Tenets and Rules of The First Church of Christ, Scientist, in Boston, Mass., is eligible to membership.

To The First Church of Christ, Scientist, in Boston, Mass.

Robert H. Mitchell, Clerk.

I hereby make application for membership, and subscribe to the Tenets and the By-Laws of the Church.

My teacher in Christian Science is

————————— *James B. Brown, C.S.D.* —————————

I am not a member of any church.

Application I — *(Continued)*

PROPERLY SIGNED AND ENDORSED, ACCORDING TO ARTICLE V, SECT. 2

FORM 1, — *(Continued.)*

I was formerly a member of the _____ _____ denomination,

but have definitely severed my connection therewith.

Name _____ Mrs. Jennie W. Field, C.S. _____

Street and Number _____ 18 Forest St., _____

Town or City _____ Chicago, _____

State _____ Ill. _____

Date _____ Jan. 2nd, 1901. _____

I cordially approve the applicant.

(a) _____ James B. Brown, C.S.D. _____

Countersigned by _____

DO NOT DETACH.

TO THE APPLICANT: Name _____ Mrs. Jennie W. Field, C.S., _____

Please fill out the following for the use of the Treasurer of the Church:

Street and Number _____ 18 Forest St., _____

Town or City _____ Chicago, _____

State _____ Ill. _____

Application I

PROPERLY SIGNED AND ENDORSED, ACCORDING TO ARTICLE V, SECT. 2

If you have been taught by a loyal student who has taken a degree at the Massachusetts Metaphysical College, or by one who has passed an examination by the Board of Education, fill this blank.

FORM 1.

The First Church of Christ, Scientist, in Boston, Mass., is designed to be built on the rock of Christ — Truth and Life — and to reflect the Church Triumphant.

One who is not a member of any church, excepting a branch church of Christ, Scientist, who loves Christian Science, and reads understandingly the Bible, and SCIENCE AND HEALTH WITH KEY TO THE SCRIPTURES, by Reverend Mary Baker Eddy, and other works by this author, and who is Christianly qualified and can enter into full fellowship with the Tenets and Rules of The First Church of Christ, Scientist, in Boston, Mass., is eligible to membership.

To The First Church of Christ, Scientist, in Boston, Mass.

Robert H. Mitchell, Clerk.

I hereby make application for membership, and subscribe to the Tenets and the By-Laws of the Church.

My teacher in Christian Science is

_____ *James B. Brown, C.S.D.* _____

I am not a member of any church, ~~excepting~~ _____
~~Church of Christ, Scientist, at~~ _____

Application I — (Continued)

PROPERLY SIGNED AND ENDORSED, ACCORDING TO ARTICLE V, SECT. 2

FORM 1, — (Continued.)

I was formerly a member of the _____ _____ denomination, but have definitely severed my connection therewith.

Name _____ Mrs. Jennie W. Field, C.S. _____

Street and Number _____ 18 Forest St., _____

Town or City _____ Chicago, _____

State _____ Ill. _____

Date _____ Jan. 2nd, 1901. _____

I cordially approve this applicant.

(a) _____ James B. Brown, C.S.D. _____

Countersigned by _____

DO NOT DETACH.

TO THE APPLICANT: Name _____ Mrs. Jennie W. Field, C.S., _____

Please fill out the following for the use of the Treasurer of the Church:

Street and Number _____ 18 Forest St., _____

Town or City _____ Chicago, _____

State _____ Ill. _____

Application II

FORM 2.

One who is not a member of any church, excepting a branch church of Christ, Scientist, who loves Christian Science, and reads understandingly the Bible, and SCIENCE AND HEALTH WITH KEY TO THE SCRIPTURES, by Reverend Mary Baker Eddy, and other works by this author, and who is Christianly qualified and can enter into full fellowship with the Tenets and Rules of The First Church of Christ, Scientist, in Boston, Mass., is eligible to membership.

To The First Church of Christ, Scientist, in Boston, Mass.

Robert H. Mitchell, Clerk.

I hereby make application for membership, and subscribe to the Tenets and the By-Laws of the Church. I have not studied Christian Science with a teacher, and am not a member of any church excepting *Second* Church of Christ, Scientist, at *New York, N. Y.*

I was formerly a member of the _____

_____ denomination,

but have definitely severed my connection therewith.

If you have not been taught by a loyal student who has taken a degree at the Massachusetts Metaphysical College, or by one who has passed an examination by the Board of Education, fill this blank.

Application II — *(Continued)*

SIGNED, ENDORSED, AND COUNTERSIGNED, ACCORDING TO ARTICLE VI, SECT. 2

FORM 2, — *(Continued.)*

Name _____ *Miss Emma L. French* _____

Street and Number _____ *293 Emerson St.,* _____

Town or City _____ *New York* _____

State _____ *N. Y.* _____

Date _____ *Jan. 2nd, 1901.* _____

I cordially approve this applicant.

(a) _____ *Miss Mary E. Grant, C.S.* _____

Countersigned by _____ *James B. Brown, C.S.D.* _____

DO NOT DETACH

TO THE APPLICANT: Name _____ *Miss Emma L. French* _____

Please fill out the following for the use of the Treasurer of the Church: Street and Number _____ *293 Emerson St.* _____

Town or City _____ *New York* _____

State _____ *N. Y.* _____

Present Order of Services in
The Mother Church and Branch Churches

Republished from the Sentinel

SUNDAY SERVICES

1. Hymn.
2. Reading a Scriptural Selection.
3. Silent Prayer, followed by the audible repetition of the Lord's Prayer with its spiritual interpretation.
4. Hymn.
5. Announcing necessary notices.
6. Solo.
7. Reading the Explanatory Note on first leaf of *Quarterly*.
8. Announcing the subject of the Lesson-Sermon, and reading the Golden Text.
9. Reading the Scriptural Selection, entitled "Responsive Reading," alternately by the First Reader and the congregation.
10. Reading the Lesson-Sermon. (After the Second Reader reads the BIBLE references of

the first Section of the Lesson, the First Reader makes the following announcement: "As announced in the explanatory note, I shall now read correlative passages from the Christian Science textbook, SCIENCE AND HEALTH WITH KEY TO THE SCRIPTURES, by Mary Baker Eddy.")

11.   Collection.

12.   Hymn.

13.   Reading the Scientific Statement of Being, and the correlative SCRIPTURE according to I John 3:1-3.

14.   Pronouncing Benediction.

The services should be preceded and followed by organ or piano music of an appropriate character in all cases where this is possible.

On the first Sunday of each month Article VIII, SECT. 1, *A Rule for Motives and Acts,* is to be read.

WEDNESDAY MEETINGS

1. Hymn.
2. Reading from the BIBLE, and correlative passages from SCIENCE AND HEALTH WITH KEY TO THE SCRIPTURES.
3. Silent Prayer, followed by the audible repetition of the Lord's Prayer, its spiritual interpretation being omitted.
4. Hymn.
5. Announcing necessary notices.
6. Experiences, testimonies, and remarks on Christian Science.
7. Closing Hymn.

The services should be preceded and followed by organ or piano music of an appropriate character in all cases where this is possible.

Thanksgiving Day

*Order of Service for The Mother Church and
Branch Churches*

1. Hymn.

2. Reading the Thanksgiving Proclamation of the President of the United States, or the Governor of the state, or both.

3. Reading a Scriptural Selection.

4. Silent Prayer, followed by the audible repetition of the Lord's Prayer with its spiritual interpretation.

5. Hymn.

6. Reading the Explanatory Note on the first leaf of the *Quarterly*.

7. Announcing the subject of the Lesson-Sermon, and reading the Golden Text.

8. Responsive Reading by the First Reader and the congregation.

9. Reading the Lesson-Sermon prepared by the Bible Lesson Committee.

10. Solo.

11. Testimonies by Christian Scientists, appropriate for the occasion.

12. Hymn.

13. Reading the Scientific Statement of Being, and the correlative SCRIPTURE according to I John 3:1-3.

14. Pronouncing Benediction.

No collection is to be taken at this service.

The services should be preceded and followed by organ or piano music of an appropriate character in all cases where this is possible.

Present Order of Communion Services in Branch Churches

1. Hymn.
2. Reading a Scriptural Selection.
3. Silent Prayer, followed by the audible repetition of the Lord's Prayer with its spiritual interpretation.
4. Hymn.
5. Announcing necessary notices.
6. Reading Tenets of The Mother Church.
7. Collection and Solo.
8. Reading the Explanatory Note on first leaf of *Quarterly.*
9. Announcing the subject of the Lesson-Sermon, and reading the Golden Text.
10. Reading the Scriptural Selection entitled "Responsive Reading" alternately by the First Reader and the congregation.
11. Reading the Lesson-Sermon. (After the Second Reader reads the BIBLE references of the first Section of the Lesson, the First Reader

makes the following announcement: "As announced in the explanatory note, I shall now read correlative passages from the Christian Science textbook, SCIENCE AND HEALTH WITH KEY TO THE SCRIPTURES, by Mary Baker Eddy.")

12.   The First Reader briefly invites the congregation to kneel in silent Communion. This is concluded by the audible repetition of the Lord's Prayer (spiritual interpretation omitted).

13.   Singing the Doxology:

> "Be Thou, O God, exalted high;
> And as Thy glory fills the sky,
> So let it be on earth displayed,
> Till Thou art here and now obeyed."

14.   Reading the Scientific Statement of Being and the correlative SCRIPTURE according to I John 3:1-3.

15.   Pronouncing Benediction.

The Church Tenets shall be read at this service.

The services should be preceded and followed by organ or piano music of an appropriate character in all cases where this is possible.

Order of Exercises for the Sunday School of The Mother Church and Branch Churches[1]

1. Call to order by the Superintendent.
2. Hymn.
3. Subject of the lesson announced; Golden Text repeated by the children; Responsive Reading.
4. Silent prayer, followed by the audible repetition of the Lord's Prayer in unison.
5. Instruction in classes, in accordance with Sections 2 and 3 of Article XX of the Manual of The Mother Church.
6. Entire school reassembles.
7. Hymn.
8. Scientific Statement of Being read by the Superintendent.
9. School dismissed.

[1] If a collection is taken, it should be taken in the classes before they reassemble.

Deed of Trust

*The following is a Copy of the Deed of Trust
Conveying Land for Church Edifice*

KNOW ALL MEN BY THESE PRESENTS,

That I Mary Baker G. Eddy of Concord in
the County of Merrimack and State of New
Hampshire in consideration of one dollar to
me paid by Ira O. Knapp of Boston, Massachusetts, William B. Johnson of Boston,
Massachusetts, Joseph S. Eastaman of Chel-
sea, Massachusetts, and Stephen A. Chase of
Fall River, Massachusetts, the receipt whereof
is hereby acknowledged, and, also in consideration of the trusts and uses hereinafter mentioned and established, do hereby give, bargain,
sell, and convey to the said Ira O. Knapp, William B. Johnson, Joseph S. Eastaman, and
Stephen A. Chase as trustees as hereinafter
provided and to their legitimate successors in

office forever, a certain parcel of land situate on Falmouth street in said Boston, bounded and described as follows: Beginning at the junction of Falmouth street, and a forty-foot street now called Caledonia street; thence running Southwest on said Falmouth street one hundred and sixteen and eighty-eight hundredths feet; thence Northwest at a right angle to a point where a line drawn at right angles to said forty-foot street at a point thereon one hundred and sixteen and fifty-five hundredths feet Northwest from the point of beginning meets the said boundary at right angles to Falmouth street, sixty-six and seventy-eight hundredths feet; thence at an obtuse angle on said line at right angles to said forty-foot street sixty-seven and thirty-five hundredths feet to said forty-foot street; thence Southeasterly on said forty-foot street one hundred and sixteen and fifty-five hundredths feet to the point of beginning; containing seven thousand eight hundred and twenty-eight square feet more or less, and subject to the agreements and restrictions mentioned in a deed recorded in Suffolk Registry of Deeds Lib. 1719, Fol. 83 so far as the same are now legally operative.

This deed of conveyance is made upon the following express trusts and conditions which the said grantees by accepting this deed agree and covenant for themselves and their successors in office to fully perform and fulfil.

1. Said grantees shall be known as the "Christian Science Board of Directors," and shall constitute a perpetual body or corporation under and in accordance with section one, Chapter 39 of the Public Statutes of Massachusetts.[1] Whenever a vacancy occurs in said Board the remaining members shall within thirty days fill the same by election; but no one shall be eligible to that office who is not in the opinion of the remaining members of the Board a firm and consistent believer in the doctrines of Christian Science as taught in a book entitled "SCIENCE AND HEALTH," by Mary Baker G. Eddy beginning with the seventy-first edition thereof.

[1] The deacons, church wardens, or other similar officers of churches or religious societies, and the trustees of the Methodist Episcopal churches, appointed according to the discipline and usages thereof, shall, if citizens of this commonwealth, be deemed bodies corporate for the purpose of taking and holding in succession all grants and donations, whether of real or personal estate, made either to them and their successors, or to their respective churches, or to the poor of their churches.

Editor's note: In May 1971, this statute (renumbered section one of Chapter 68) was amended by substituting "residents" for "citizens."

2. Said Board shall within five years from the date hereof build or cause to be built upon said lot of land a suitable and convenient church edifice, the cost of which shall not be less than fifty thousand dollars.

3. When said church building is completed said Board shall elect a pastor, reader or speaker to fill the pulpit who shall be a genuine Christian Scientist; they shall maintain public worship in accordance with the doctrines of Christian Science in said church, and for this purpose they are fully empowered to make any and all necessary rules and regulations.

4. Said Board of Directors shall not suffer or allow any building to be erected upon said lot except a church building or edifice, nor shall they allow said church building or any part thereof to be used for any other purpose than for the ordinary and usual uses of a church.

5. Said Board of Directors shall not allow or permit in said church building any preaching or other religious services which shall not be consonant and in strict harmony with the doctrines and practice of Christian Science as taught and explained by Mary Baker G. Eddy in the seventy-

first edition of her book entitled "SCIENCE AND HEALTH," which is soon to be issued, and in any subsequent edition thereof.

6. The congregation which shall worship in said church shall be styled "The First Church of Christ, Scientist."

7. Said Directors shall not sell or mortgage the land hereby conveyed; but they shall see that all taxes and legal assessments on said property are promptly paid.

8. Said church building shall not be removed from said lot except for the purpose of rebuilding thereon a more expensive or a more convenient structure in which said doctrines of Christian Science only shall be preached and practised. If said church building is removed for either of the purposes above set forth, any and all tablets and inscriptions which are or shall be upon said church building at the time of removal shall be removed therefrom and placed upon the walls of the new edifice. If said building is burned, the Directors shall forthwith proceed to rebuild the church.

9. Said Directors shall maintain regular preaching, reading or speaking in said church

on each Sabbath, and an omission to have and maintain such preaching, reading or speaking for one year in succession shall be deemed a breach of this condition.

10. Whenever said Directors shall determine that it is inexpedient to maintain preaching, reading or speaking in said church in accordance with the terms of this deed, they are authorized and required to reconvey forthwith said lot of land with the building thereon to Mary Baker G. Eddy, her heirs and assigns forever by a proper deed of conveyance.

11. The omission or neglect on the part of said Directors to strictly comply with any of the conditions herein contained shall constitute a breach thereof, and the title hereby conveyed shall revert to the grantor Mary Baker G. Eddy, her heirs and assigns forever, upon her entry upon said land and taking possession thereof for such breach.

To Have and to Hold the above granted premises with all the privileges and appurtenances thereon belonging to said grantees and their successors in office to the uses and trusts above described forever.

And the said grantor for herself and her heirs, executors and administrators covenants with the said grantees and their successors in office that she is lawfully seized in fee simple of the aforesaid premises, that they are free from all incumbrances not herein mentioned or referred to, that she has good right to sell and convey the same to the said grantees and their successors in office as aforesaid, and that she will and her heirs, executors, and administrators shall, warrant and defend the same to the said grantees and their successors in office forever against the lawful claims and demands of all persons.

In witness whereof I the said Mary Baker G. Eddy have hereto set my hand and seal this 1st day of September, 1892.

MARY BAKER G. EDDY.

Signed, sealed, and delivered in presence of

LAURA E. SARGENT.
R. E. WALKER.

September 1st, 1892.

STATE OF NEW HAMPSHIRE, }
        MERRIMACK. } *ss.*

Then personally appeared the above named Mary Baker G. Eddy and acknowledged the foregoing instrument to be her free act and deed,

Before me

R. E. WALKER.
Notary Public.

September 2, 1892.

SUFFOLK REGISTRY OF DEEDS, Lib. 2081, Fol. 257.

Deed Conveying Land for
Church Purposes

METCALF *to* KNAPP *et al. Trs.*
Libro 2886, Fol. 521.

KNOW ALL MEN,

That I, Albert Metcalf, the grantor in a certain deed given to Ira O. Knapp and others dated October 23, 1896, and recorded with Suffolk Deeds, Book 2591, page 398, do hereby declare that the land conveyed by said deed was conveyed to the grantees therein, as they are the Christian Science Board of Directors, upon the trusts, but not subject to the conditions mentioned in the deed creating said Board given by Mary Baker G. Eddy to Ira O. Knapp and others, dated September 1st, 1892, and recorded with Suffolk Deeds, Book 2081, page 257. In addition to the trusts contained in said deed of September 1, 1892, from Mary Baker G. Eddy, this property is conveyed on the further trusts that no new Tenet or By-Law shall be adopted, nor any Tenet or By-Law amended or annulled by the grantees unless the written consent of said Mary Baker G. Eddy, the author of the textbook "SCIENCE AND HEALTH WITH KEY TO THE SCRIPTURES," be given therefor, or unless at the written request of Mrs. Eddy the Executive Members of The First Church of Christ, Scientist, (formerly called the "First Members,") by a two-thirds vote of all their number, decide so to do. And that the same inscription which is on the outside of the present church edifice shall be placed on any new church erected on said lot. And in consideration of one dollar to me paid by said Ira O. Knapp, William B. Johnson, Joseph Armstrong and Stephen A. Chase, the receipt whereof is hereby acknowledged, I do hereby confirm the deed as above mentioned, and do grant and release unto them, their heirs, successors and assigns in trust as aforesaid, the premises therein described.

In Witness Whereof I have hereunto set my hand and seal this nineteenth day of March, A. D. nineteen hundred and three.

ALBERT METCALF. [Seal]

Commonwealth of Massachusetts
    Suffolk } *ss.* March 20th, 1903.

Then said Albert Metcalf acknowledged the foregoing instrument to be his free act and deed.

Before me

Malcolm McLoud.
Justice of the Peace.

March 20, 1903, at twelve o'clock and sixteen minutes p. m. Received, Entered and Examined.

Attest: Thos. F. Temple, *Reg.*

A true copy from the Records of Deeds for the County of Suffolk, Lib. 2886, Fol. 521.

Attest: Chas. W. Kimball, *Asst. Reg.*